ARMANDO'S ISLAND

Text copyright © 2023 by Marsha Diane Arnold
Illustrations copyright © 2023 by Anne Yvonne Gilbert
Edited by Kate Riggs / Designed by Rita Marshall
Published in 2023 by Creative Editions
P.O. Box 227, Mankato, MN 56002 USA
Creative Editions is an imprint of The Creative Company
www.thecreativecompany.us

Library of Congress Cataloging-in-Publication Data
Names: Arnold, Marsha Diane, author. / Gilbert, Yvonne, illustrator.
Title: Armando's island / by Marsha Diane Arnold; illustrated by Anne Yvonne Gilbert.
Summary: Reflecting an ethos that we are called to be caretakers of a planet in
precarious balance, this lush picture book reflects the strikingly biodiverse
environment of the Amazon rainforest.
Identifiers: LCCN 2022048902 (print) / LCCN 2022048903 (ebook) /
ISBN 9781568463766 (hardcover) / ISBN 9781640006751 (ebook)
Subjects: LCSH: Deforestation—Amazon River Region—Juvenile literature. /
Rainforest animals—Habitat—Conservation—Amazon River Region—Juvenile literature. /
Rainforest ecology—Amazon River Region—Juvenile literature.
Classification: LCC SD418.3.A53 A76 2023 (print) / LCC SD418.3.A53 (ebook)
DDC 333.750981/1—dc23/eng/20221115
LC record available at https://lccn.loc.gov/2022048902
LC ebook record available at https://lccn.loc.gov/2022048903
First edition 9 8 7 6 5 4 3 2 1

MARSHA DIANE ARNOLD & ANNE YVONNE GILBERT

ARMANDO'S ISLAND

CREATIVE EDITIONS

Beneath a canopy of trees, flowing like green ocean,

in an ancient forest,

lived Armando.

Each morning he awakened to the smell of the earth,

the sounds and songs of treetops,

the taste of just-picked berries.

He grew to know the moods of the rainforest—

the angry thunder,

the endless rain,

the deep darkness of the forest floor,

the sunlight snaking its way through a bright gap,

where a giant tree had fallen.

Walking barefoot, leaves crunching beneath him,

playing along riverbanks, mud squishing between toes,

skipping across fallen logs, grasshoppers jumping,

climbing liana vines, lizards scrambling beside him,

he felt connected to his leafy refuge.

As time passed, Armando's legs skipped

less and climbed more carefully.

But with the first song of the toucan,

he remembered:

Chasing butterflies along a golden stream,

calling to howler monkeys swinging high above,

dancing to the rain's rhythm with a leaf as his umbrella.

One day, a tree cutter came to Armando.

"We need these trees to build houses and furniture.

Your land will make you rich."

"I am rich already," said Armando,

gazing at the emerald garden surrounding him.

So the tree cutter took his money to Armando's

neighbor in the north.

In the morning, to the north, the whir of chainsaws

and groan of bulldozers

shook the earth.

Macaws stopped screeching.

Monkeys stopped swinging.

Tree frogs stopped splashing.

Green-furred sloths opened sleepy, saucer eyes,

as they fled, to the south, to Armando's.

oon after, a man and woman came to Armando.

"We need your land for a cattle ranch.

We will give you whatever you ask."

"I ask nothing. The forest provides all," said Armando,
plucking ripe fruit from a tree.

So the couple went to Armando's neighbor in the south.

In the morning, to the south, rushing flames
and clouds of smoke crowded the sky.

Beetles stopped crunching.

Boas stopped twining.

Ocelots stopped prowling.

Agoutis left their half-chewed seeds,

as they fled, to the north, to Armando's.

Some time later, city dwellers came to Armando.

"Armando, you are a powerful man.

You own land from which more power will come.

On your river, we will build a giant dam."

"There is power also in the small," said Armando,

watching two butterflies dart between the flowers.

So the city dwellers went to Armando's neighbor in the east.

In the morning, to the east, a great hammering

and sharp drilling

wailed through the air.

Dolphins stopped swimming.

Otters stopped sliding.

Capybaras stopped bathing.

Hummingbirds left their dance beneath the waterfall

as they fled, to the west, to Armando's.

In time, a crowd came to Armando.

"Riches lie beneath your land—copper, nickel, and gold.

You have refused money, gifts, and power,

but we have something we know you will want.

Far from this ancient forest is a place with more land

and many more animals and plants to shelter.

We will trade you that great piece of land for this small one."

Agoutis stopped chewing and listened.

Sloths opened their eyes and watched.

Hummingbirds stilled their wings and waited.

And Armando remembered:

Chasing butterflies along a golden stream,

calling to howler monkeys swinging high above,

dancing to the rain's rhythm with a leaf as his umbrella.

"One piece of land cannot be traded for another," he told the crowd.

"Each piece has its own treasures to give."

So the crowd went to Armando's neighbor in the west.

The next morning, to the west, a great scar was cut in the forest.

Jewel-coated frogs stopped croaking.

Golden kinkajous stopped chattering.

Copper-colored monkeys stopped climbing.

And the solitary jaguar joined the others

as they fled, to the east, to Armando's.

Now, Armando's home stands crowded and apart,

an island of emerald green, shimmering in the sunlight.

Sometimes the people to the north, south, east, and west

glance at Armando's island, fragile in the mist.

Armando hopes that some morning with the first song of the toucan,

a long-ago memory will come to them ...

Chasing butterflies along a golden stream,

calling to howler monkeys swinging high above,

dancing to the rain's rhythm with a leaf as their umbrella.

ANIMALS OF THE AMAZON RAINFOREST

Scientists usually study rainforests in four layers. This story focuses first on the canopy and emergent trees and animals that live there, then the understory and forest floor, and finally, the river. Many of the animals can be found in more than one layer, but they usually prefer one over another.

1) Emergent, where trees rise to 200 feet above the canopy and their trunks can reach 16 feet wide
2) Canopy, where trees can grow 100 to 150 feet tall
3) Understory, where only about 5 percent of sunlight reaches
4) Forest floor, where the soil is poor
5) Amazon River

Toco toucans nest in tree cavities in the canopy and are very vocal and social birds. Indigenous peoples regard toucans as sacred birds.

Butterflies in the Amazon rainforest are active year round. Clouds of butterflies can sometimes be seen as they feed along sandbars and fly over rivers.

Howler monkeys live in the emergent layer and almost never come down from the trees. Male howler monkeys have a pouch in their throat that is like a megaphone. Their calls can be heard up to three miles away, announcing their claim to territory.

Scarlet macaws nest in the hollow trunks of palm trees, preferring life in the canopy. Their strong beak cracks nuts and seeds.

Canopy-dwelling **spider monkeys** screech and bark to communicate. They help spread seeds by eating fruit in one tree and defecating the seeds elsewhere.

Tree frogs are found in the canopy, relatively safe from predators. They have sticky pads on their feet that allow them to climb up and down trees. After their eggs hatch, some tree frogs move their tadpoles into water pockets that gather in the leaves of plants like bromeliads.

Three-toed sloths sleep most of the day in the canopy of the rainforest. When they awaken, they move so slowly that algae grow on their coats, making their fur look gray-green.

Scientists once found 700 different species of **beetle** on a single Amazonian tree! One amazing species is the titan beetle, perhaps the world's largest beetle at a length of up to six and a half inches.

Amazon Basin emerald tree boas live in the forests and wetlands along the Amazon River. They can live fairly close to the ground but are also found in the canopy. These nonvenomous snakes are solitary and nocturnal, growing to nine feet long.

The **ocelot** is the third largest cat in South America, after the jaguar and puma (mountain lion). Ocelots are mostly active at night, hunting birds, fish, and small mammals. During the day, they often sleep in thick vegetation on the ground, but they may climb up to the canopy trees to rest.

Agoutis are the only known animal with teeth strong enough to break open the tough Brazil nut pod. They store the seeds beneath the soil, dig them up, and rebury them again and again, a behavior called "scatterhoard." It is beneficial to both agoutis and trees, as the seeds may sprout and grow into new trees, which will feed more agoutis.

Pink river dolphins are unique because of their pink color and flexible necks that allow them to move their heads from left to right. They are threatened by river pollution and hydroelectric projects that restrict the river's natural flow.

The **giant river otter**, which grows up to about six feet long, including a nearly three-foot tail, is found in three river systems: the Amazon, Orinoco, and La Plata. Its webbed paws are perfect for swimming and hunting in slow-flowing tributaries.

Capybaras, often found near lakes and rivers, love the water and are sociable animals. They are the largest rodents in the world, with males being 4 feet long and weighing as much as 140 pounds. Their name means "grass-eater" in the language of the Tupi people.

Hummingbirds are some of the rainforest's busiest animals. They must consume about half their weight in sugar daily. Their wings flap up to 80 beats per second, and their hearts beat more than 1,200 times per minute. Hummingbirds in the Amazon are frequently seen hovering over flowers and lapping up nectar with their long, hollow tongues.

Poison frogs are known as jewels of the rainforest, as their skin comes in sparkling colors—yellow and green, orange and silver, blue and yellow. These beautiful colors are actually a warning to other animals not to touch or eat them.

Red uakari have a copper-colored coat (reddish-brown to orange). They live only in the Amazon basin, preferring flooded rainforest near small rivers and lakes.

Kinkajous are nocturnal and spend most of their waking hours in the canopy. They enjoy drinking the nectar of flowers; their diet is 90 percent fruit.

Jaguars spend most of their time on the forest floor, but they are excellent climbers and good swimmers. Jaguars are called an "umbrella species" because if large areas of land are protected for *their* survival, other species are likewise protected.

There are many varieties of **fruit** that grow in the rainforest. Some are familiar, like bananas and coconuts. Lesser known (outside South America) examples are passion fruit and bacaba, a dark red or purple fruit, the juice of which is a popular drink in Brazil.

Many Amazonian **plants** hold medicinal value, and new ones are being discovered each year. On average, explorers are finding a new species of plant or animal every other day. If the rainforest is destroyed, we will never know how some of these species could help the world.